CATS OF JAPAN
WOODBLOCK PRINTS BY HOKUSAI, HIROSHIGE AND OTHER ARTISTS

I0418849

CATS OF JAPAN
WOODBLOCK PRINTS BY HOKUSAI, HIROSHIGE AND OTHER ARTISTS

JOCELYN BOUQUILLARD

PRESTEL
MUNICH • LONDON • NEW YORK

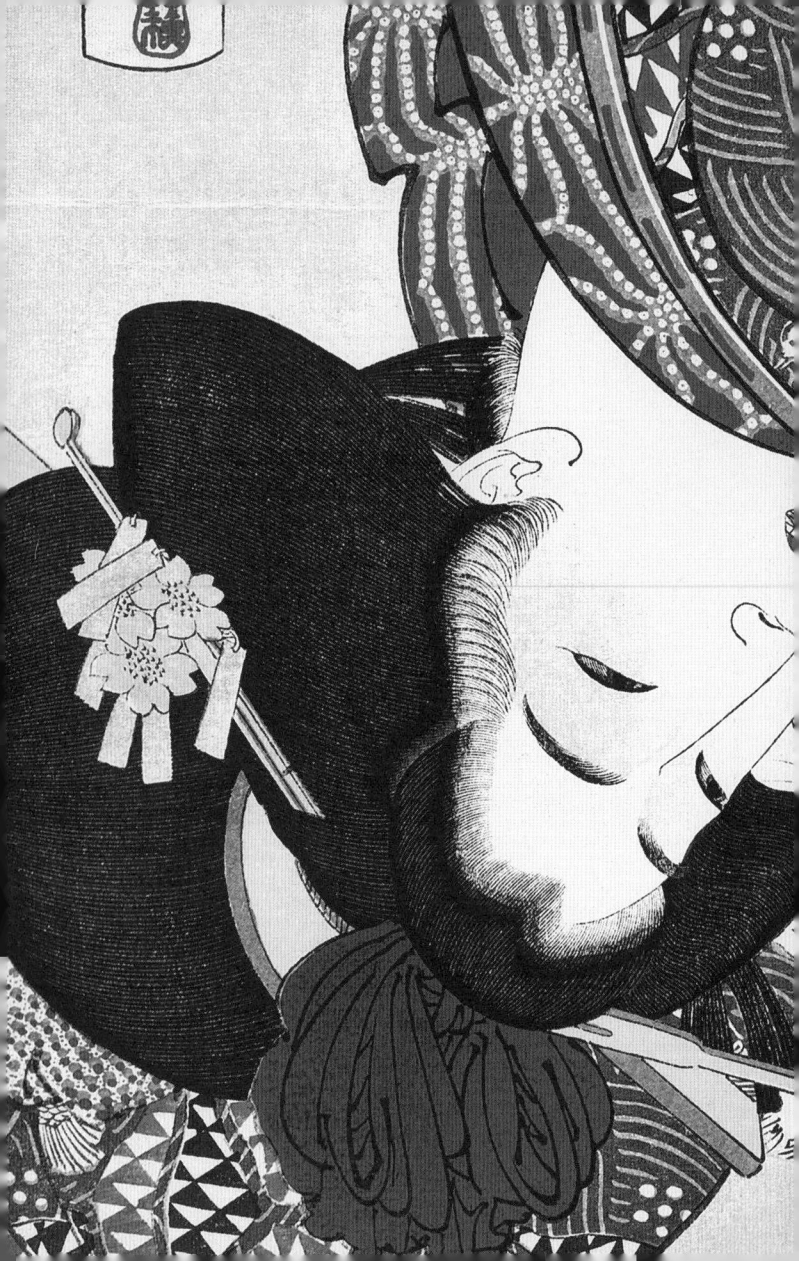

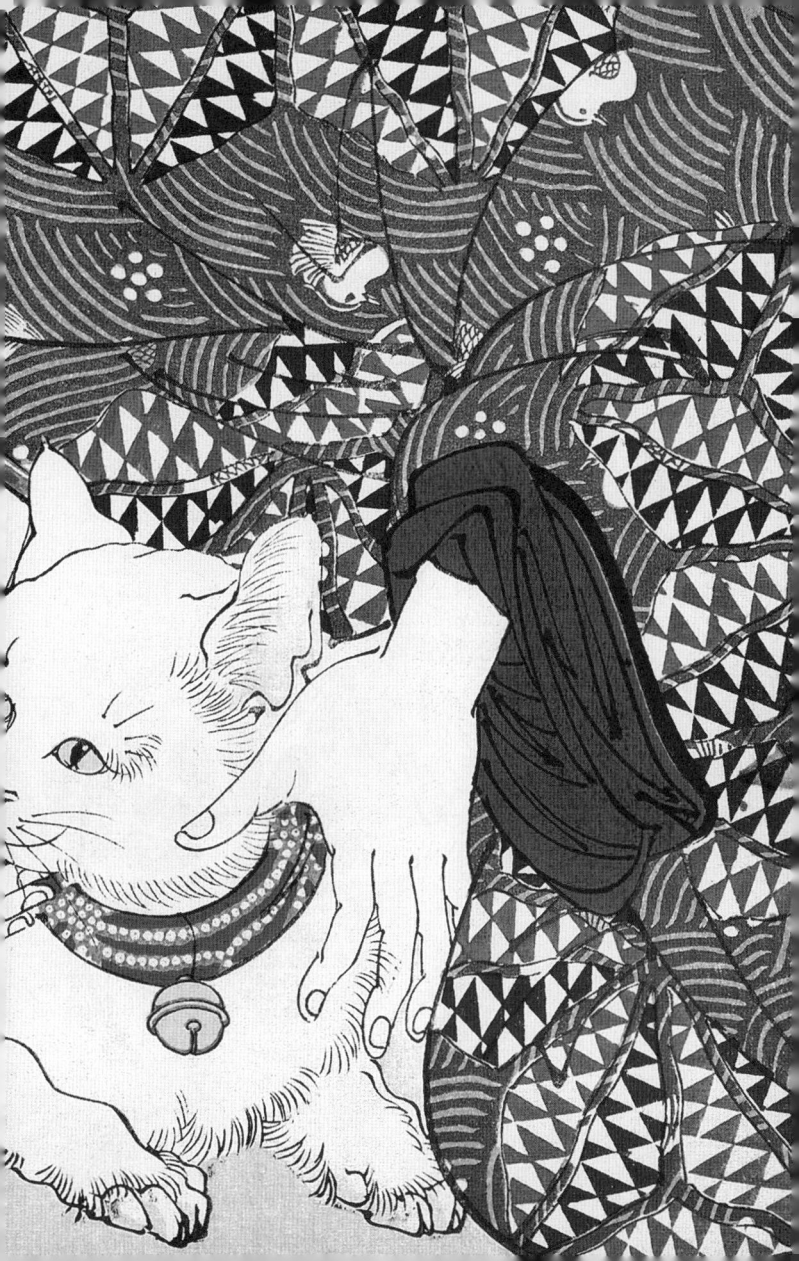

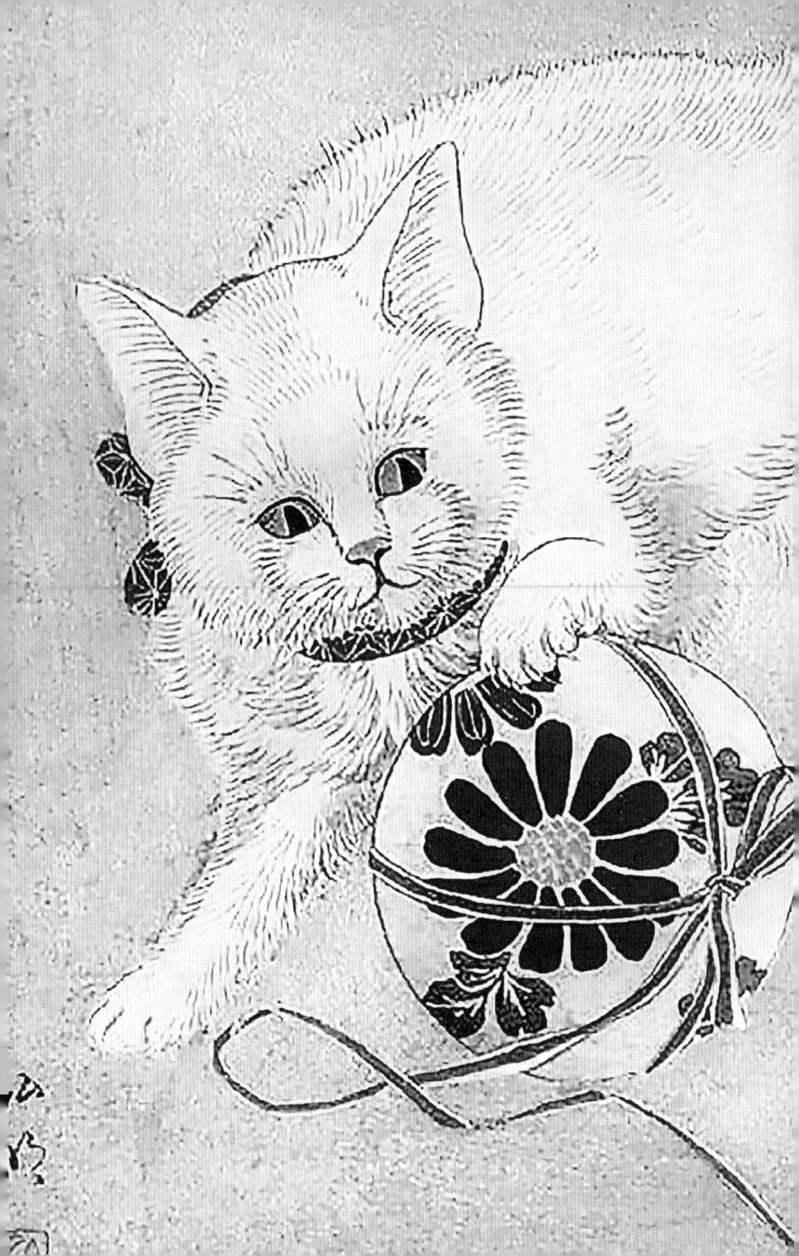

In Japan, cats are of paramount importance. As in ancient Egypt, they are venerated, adored and even idolised. Most often perceived as a good luck charm (the *maneki-neko*), cats can also play an evil role (the *bakeneko* – a monstrous cat, a vampire and a sorcerer). This binary symbolism can be explained by these mysterious, enigmatic, fascinating and elusive felines' ambiguous behaviour; by turns gentle and devious, playful and independent, bewitchingly beautiful, cats are also capable of unpredictable – even cruel – reactions.

Appearing in folklore and Kabuki plays, and a recurring theme in poetry, they also feature in Japanese *ukiyo-e* prints (in the 18th and 19th centuries) and more modern Meiji prints. Cats are very often depicted in the company of women, snuggled up in their arms, playing with them or napping beside them. Some prints, where they are depicted in the posture of a predator, highlight their protective role against rodents. They can also be a symbol of eroticism, particularly when represented in *shunga* and in the company of geishas. Lastly, they sometimes appear personified in human activities and attitudes, or transfigured in monstrous forms.

A playful pet, a bringer of good luck and a hunter

A beneficial spirit, the *maneki-neko* (literally, "beckoning cat") wards off misfortune and illness and brings good luck, happiness and wealth. A Buddhist temple in Tokyo, the Gotoku-ji, is dedicated to this figure; it contains hundreds of statuettes of benevolent cats, while in the countryside, shrines and stone effigies are built to them, imploring them to protect crops from rodents.

This embodiment of good luck is underpinned by two legends: according to the first, a man, intrigued by a cat waving at him, approached it; suddenly, a bolt of lightning struck the exact spot where the man was standing a few seconds before. The man was therefore saved by the cat's beckoning gesture. The other legend tells the story of the courtesan Usugumo, captured in a number of prints, notably by Tsukioka Yoshitoshi (pl. 59). This geisha, who lived in the Yoshiwara District in the east of Tokyo, was surprised one night by the attitude of her cat, who would not stop tugging at her kimono. Seeing this, the owner of the brothel believed the cat to be bewitched, and beheaded it. Thrown with force, the cat's head crushed a snake that was about to bite. To comfort Usugumo, who was devastated by the death of her cat, a customer had a wooden statue carved the cat's likeness, which became the first *maneki-neko*. Ceramic or porcelain statuettes, often displayed in the windows of Japanese stores, teahouses and restaurants as mascots welcoming customers, depict the *maneki-neko* in the form of a cat raising its left paw, or both front paws, up to its ears.

The first written record of the presence of a cat in Japan mentions that on 19 September 999, the Korean emperor Ichijo presented a cat to the Japanese imperial family. Cats from China had likely been introduced to the Japanese archipelago several centuries earlier. They are thought to have appeared there concomitantly with the arrival of Buddhist thought: Chinese ships carrying religious texts were required to have cats on board, to prevent rodents from eating the precious documents.

During the Middle Ages, and up until the 18th century, cats were luxury animals, and quite rare, reserved for an elite that could afford them.

Their company was particularly popular with high society women, becoming their pet of choice; the ladies of the imperial court and the upper caste held them on a leash using a thin, supple red silk ribbon, as depicted in prints by Kunisada (pl. 51) and Harunobu (pl. 25), illustrating *The Tale of Genji*, a masterpiece of 11th-century Japanese literature recounting the life of Prince Genji at the imperial court in Kyoto. The works of art show these remarkably pampered and adored domestic cats living in the idleness and luxury of aristocratic homes.

Originally, and for several centuries, cats were held captive inside the homes of the Japanese upper classes; from the 17th century onwards, however, they were set free to follow their hunting instincts, ridding the streets and fields of the mice and rats swarming them, ravaging goods and produce and causing considerable damage to silk production. With a decree in 1602, the government made their captivity illegal and prohibited their trade, because of their natural aptitude for hunting – and therefore, their usefulness as predators of rodents. Cats protected both rice harvests and silkworm cocoons; they kept manuscripts safe from mice, preventing rodents from nibbling Buddhist scrolls inside temples. According to custom, to this end, each shrine had to be home to at least two cats.

Woodblock prints often bear witness to the cats' more utilitarian role. They depict rats and mice being chased by cats, playing cruelly with their prey, as represented by Kyōsai (pl. 74), Kiyochika (pl. 36) and Koson (pl. 34). In some prints, they also appear to be chasing animals other than rodents, such as butterflies (*cf.* Hokkei, pl. 73, and Hokusai, pl. 61) or goldfish in an aquarium or a jar – both in the 18th century, for example in works by Koryusai (pl. 45), and in the 20th century, in prints by Koson (pl. 35 and 33).

In Edo, where houses would specialise in breeding cats, a curious speciality was born to scare off rodents: wandering artists, travelling from town to town, sold portraits of cats to residents who wished to protect their property from rodents and prevent damage caused by them. These creations, paintings of cats on scrolls or screens, vertical prints displayed on panels, served as a sort of "rodent scarecrow". Around 1842, Kuniyoshi produced a print of a *Cat to Keep Mice Away (pl. 66)* for this purpose, as the quasi-advertising commentary at the top of the plate clearly indicates: "The skilful Kuniyoshi drew this cat so faithfully that you only need to display the image in a house to scare away the mice. Their numbers will be considerably reduced, and if they do arrive, they will do no damage. This truly is a remarkable image."

This cat, bearing its claws, with its rounded back and menacing stare, indeed appears ready to pounce on its prey.

However, rodent hunting was not the only subject of attention and source of inspiration. Artists captured, with great realism, the appearance and behaviour of cats in all kinds of postures and situations, both at play and at rest; they are often depicted playing with a ball (as in prints by Chikanobu, pl. 72 and 49, along with Shotei, pl. 3), a pompom (*cf.* Sencho, pl. 50), a ribbon (*cf.* Hiroshige II, pl. 5). Sometimes, they would play with children in the middle of a hairdressing session: a cat maliciously extends a paw towards a child as their mother shaves their neck (*cf.* Kuniyoshi, pl. 69), while another attempts to escape from the arms of a little girl who is having her hair combed (*cf.* Kunisada, pl. 32). They are often depicted sleeping in a variety of positions, in their masters' and mistresses' arms or beside them (pl. 76, 56, 48, 46, 43, 42). They are particularly partial to a warm, cosy location where they can nap – the *kotatsu*, a low table placed just above the fireplace, and covered with blankets (pl. 53, 47, 22 and 8). They also enjoy cuddling sessions (pl. 59, 53, 6 and 4), and sometimes keep their mistress company while she reads (pl. 64, 57, 56). They can also observe humans while they wash or even enjoy a bath. Indeed, in this print by Toshikata Mizuno, a young woman emerging from an *onsen* (a thermal bath supplied by a hot spring) dons a splendid kimono, while her little cat looks on (pl. 70).

Among the great masters of nineteenth-century printmaking, Utagawa Kuniyoshi deserves a special mention, who considered the cat to be his favourite subject, and used it as a model in a multitude of works.

Numerous prints bear witness to his passion for cats and his intimate knowledge of their habits. Kuniyoshi often worked with a kitten on his lap or snuggled up against him, in the fold of his kimono. It is said that he kept around ten cats in his studio at all times, and that he may have had as many as fifty-three. He drew them tirelessly, endeavouring to render their playful attitudes and shifting expressions, notably in a famous triptych of 1847: *Cats Suggested as the Fifty-three Stations of the Tōkaidō Road (pl. 14)*. In 1842, he devoted a series of prints to cats, which he depicted intertwined, their contortions forming ideograms, such as the ideogram for "octopus" (pl. 16). In 1852, he used cats again in another triptych, this time to illustrate proverbs (pl. 15).

A symbol of eroticism

The word neko, which means "cat" in Japanese, has many meanings: as well as the animal, it also refers to the woman's sex and, no doubt by metonymy, to female courtesans. The presence of cats in prints therefore often conveys an erotic and libertine connotation; their gentleness evokes sensuality, and their proximity heightens the emotion and intensity of amorous games. Furthermore, this animal, which usually leaves its home to hunt at night (cf. Chikanobu, pl. 19), is associated with the night, the realm of the unconscious, dreams, fantasies, desire and eroticism. This is why cats are also very often depicted in the presence of geishas in "green houses", as can be seen, for example, in prints by Utamaro (pl. 27 and 52), Kunichika (pl. 29) and Shigenobu (pl. 26).

In this scene, the cat appears to be attentively listening to the chords his mistress is playing on her shamisen, the preferred musical instrument of courtesans: a kind of lute with a resonance box over which a cat's skin was stretched, which they used to accompany their songs. Harunobu, for his part, depicted a cat attending an erotic game: a customer is using a bamboo stick to tickle the feet of a young woman as she combs her hair and gazes at herself in two mirrors (pl. 38).

Depicting a white cat with a short tail dozing on a windowsill (pl. 20), Hiroshige placed several clues identifying the room as the bedroom of a courtesan: a mouthwash, a blue towel and bun pins decorated with artificial flowers pricked into a sheet of paper. With half-closed eyes, seated in a large window on the first floor of a Yoshiwara pleasure house, the animal is observing the landscape unfolding in the distance: a long procession is crossing the rice paddies in front of Mount Fuji, which stands out against the glowing sunset. This is a procession of pilgrims on their way to the *Torinomachi*, the Rooster Festival. The Yoshiwara was at its busiest on the day of this festival, celebrated in December: the geishas had to be present on that day and to welcome at least one customer, possibly what this cat trapped behind bars is alluding to.

As gracious relays of our indiscreet gaze, cats are quite common in *shunga* ("spring images", an expression alluding to erotic prints) at the end of the 18th century. In the position of voyeurs, eyes half-closed, they observe a couple of lovers enjoying an intimate moment. They often indulge in the same pleasures as their masters, for example in prints by Suzuki Harunobu (pl. 23) and Isoda Koryusai *(Lovers on Balcony Overlooking Two Cats Mating*, 1780).

Sometimes, they are indifferent to the scene and look away from it, as can be seen in another print by Harunobu (pl. 21). They can also play or sleep, or even protest, as in this amusing scene portrayed with humour by Katsukawa Shunsho (pl. 22): a couple are warming themselves under a duvet by a *kotatsu* (a small fireplace set into the ground with an openwork element on top, covered with a blanket). A cat, awakened from his peaceful sleep by the fire by their lovemaking, cowers and meows; gifted with speech, it protests, as stated by the dialogue transcribed in the image: "Ah, those two have disturbed my peaceful slumber! Meow, meow!"

Exceptionally, a cat may also be represented hiding what it symbolises. In a print by Utamaro (pl. 52), conveying evocative sensuality and erotic power, a young woman is depicted in a rather suggestive pose and attitude. She is half-crouching down, her head bent forward; her body is partly revealed beneath her sumptuous unbuttoned clothes, while she plays with a small cat wearing a ribbon on its head and a little bell. The female cat is folding back a piece of fabric, as if it wanted to modestly hide the anatomy of her mistress, whose gestures are concealed beneath the heap of fabrics featuring exuberant patterns.

On the contrary, in rare cases, the cat reveals its mistress's charms by slipping into her clothes. In a domestic scene depicted by Utamaro (pl. 24), a playful kitten incidentally opens the flaps of the kimono worn by a young seamstress who, seated in front of a lacquered needle box, is busy folding a fabric whose transparency reveals her bare breasts.

This is a parodic allusion to a literary theme recounted in *The Tale of Genji* (also represented by Kunisada, pl. 51, and Harunobu, pl. 25): the third princess Onna San No Miya was admired for the first time by Kashiwagi, one of the tale's heroes, when two cats, chasing each other, accidentally opened the curtain that concealed her.

Personifications and metamorphoses: anthropomorphic cats and monstrous cats

From the mid-nineteenth century onwards, Japanese prints often featured felines dressed in kimonos, adopting very human poses and attitudes, walking on two legs and going about their daily business, faithfully reflecting the activities of Edo's inhabitants. This tradition, to which we are today accustomed through albums and cartoons, originates here. Anthropomorphic cats – realistic depictions of the animals that they represented, whose faces were, however, imbued with human expressions – provided a comic touch and offered an opportunity to criticise the behaviour of the men that they caricature. The artists who resorted to these personifications demonstrate a deep understanding of human nature, a keen sense of observation and an uncompromising view of society.

Between 1841 and 1843, the reforms of the Tempō era, which enacted so-called sumptuary laws, set the backdrop for these personifications, as censorship edicts prohibited the production and distribution of prints deemed indecent or unworthy by the shogunate – particularly those representing kabuki actors, courtesans and erotic scenes. Working their way around this prohibition, certain artists (Kuniyoshi, in particular) depicted these forbidden protagonists in the guise of cats. For instance, in an 1846 print designed for an *uchiwa* fan, *Pale Moon, Cats in Season* (pl. 17), Kuniyoshi depicts a brothel for cats: customers are looking inside the brothel, where the prostitutes are waiting. Their clothes are adorned with decorative motifs inspired by cats' favourite dishes: fish, shellfish, octopus and eels. In another of Kuniyoshi's prints, three anthropomorphic feline beauties are relaxing in summer; the first is seated, playing the *shamisen*, the second is standing and holding a fan, while the third is kneeling and quenching her thirst over a basin of water (pl. 18). These cat-headed courtesans seem to have been partially metamorphosed into felines as a result of their misconduct. Cats were not the only anthropomorphised figures in Kuniyoshi's works; various animals (birds, toads, fish, foxes and others) took the place of geishas, customers, actors, politicians and bourgeois, whom the artist observed with benevolence and immortalised with genius, charm and lightness in his humorous and parodic prints.

In the 18th century appeared the dark legend of cats, the *bakeneko*, which opposed the *maneki-neko*; two main versions coexisted, that of the vampire cat of Nabeshima and that of the cat-witch of Okabe.

Here, cats are depicted as a bad omen – frightening and monstrous animals, evil spirits, cursed and sinister, capable, according to Japanese folklore, of brutally killing women, taking on their appearance and sucking the blood of their victims or even devouring them. The origin of this evil and demonic vision of cats comes from the Buddhist world, where cats were reproached for being the only animal, along with the snake, not to have been moved by the Buddha's death. While all of Buddha's disciples mourned his passing and all the animals gathered around him, the absence of the cat was noted in writings.

According to the legend of the vampire cat of Nabeshima, one night, a huge black cat (pl. 9) jumped at the throat of the Prince of Nabeshima's favourite, strangled her and took on her physical appearance in order to seduce the Prince. He failed to notice the metamorphosis and, night after night, the shape-shifting cat began to drink his blood. To release the weakened prince from her grasp, the young woman needed to be killed; once decapitated, she turned back into a big black cat, and the vampire cat's head fell to the ground.

The legend of the cat-witch of Okabe also mentions a shape-shifting cat, which was reincarnated as the ghost of a cruel, emaciated old woman who lived in this town, the twenty-second station on the Tōkaidō road connecting Edo to Kyoto. Taking on the appearance of a monstrous cat, she frightened young women to death as, at nightfall, they travelled on a pilgrimage to the temple of this station; she could even go so far as to devour travellers seeking accommodation for the night. In the end, this cat was turned into a stone.

This legend would be adapted for *kabuki* theatre; Kuniyoshi and Kunisada created fantastic sets for these plays (pl. 13 and 12), in which huge, monstrous cats fill the backdrop, their eyes glowing, their gaze cruel and their lips curled back, ready to bite; in the foreground, a cat dances alongside the old witch, wearing a pink towel on its head. Utagawa Yoshifuji, who produced a number of fragmented figures in the manner of Arcimboldo, among which *Assemblage of Kittens Form a Mother Cat* (pl. 11), produced a composite image of the monstrous mouth of this Okabe cat, composed of several interlocking cats (pl. 10).

The most common and popular breed in Japan, the Japanese bobtail, a three-coloured cat (white with black and orange spots), has a docked tail, the origin of which is also said to come from the legend of the *bakeneko*: while warming itself near a fire, a cat burnt its tail. Its tail was very long, and turned into a torch, which set fire to the whole town as the panicked animal ran through the streets. The emperor therefore decreed that all cats should have their tails cut off, to prevent such an incident from ever happening again. In reality, the bobtail's characteristically short, curled tail is the result of a recessive gene, the product of centuries of cross-breeding.

By comparing these prints with legends born from folklore and popular beliefs, one can appreciate the timeless fascination exerted by cats in Japanese culture. Sometimes loved and adored for their gentleness and beauty, sometimes feared for their cruelty and supernatural powers, cats have established themselves as an emblematic figure; they are still very often featured in a large number of cartoons and manga, as well as in everyday life and in shop windows throughout the archipelago.

In the West, at a time when the fascination for Japanese art (known as "Japonism") strongly influenced the Impressionists and various artistic movements of the last third of the 19th century, cats were frequently depicted in works inspired by Japanese prints, as evidenced by Manet's lithograph *Le Rendez-vous des Chats* (1868) and his engravings illustrating the book *Les Chats*, by Jules Champfleury (1869), in which he captured the essential characteristics of felines in a few strokes, in the manner of the Japanese masters, with an economy of gestures and simplified drawings. Prints by Théophile Steinlen – particularly his poster *La Tournée du Chat noir* (1896), for the famous Montmartre cabaret – also bear witness to this influence.

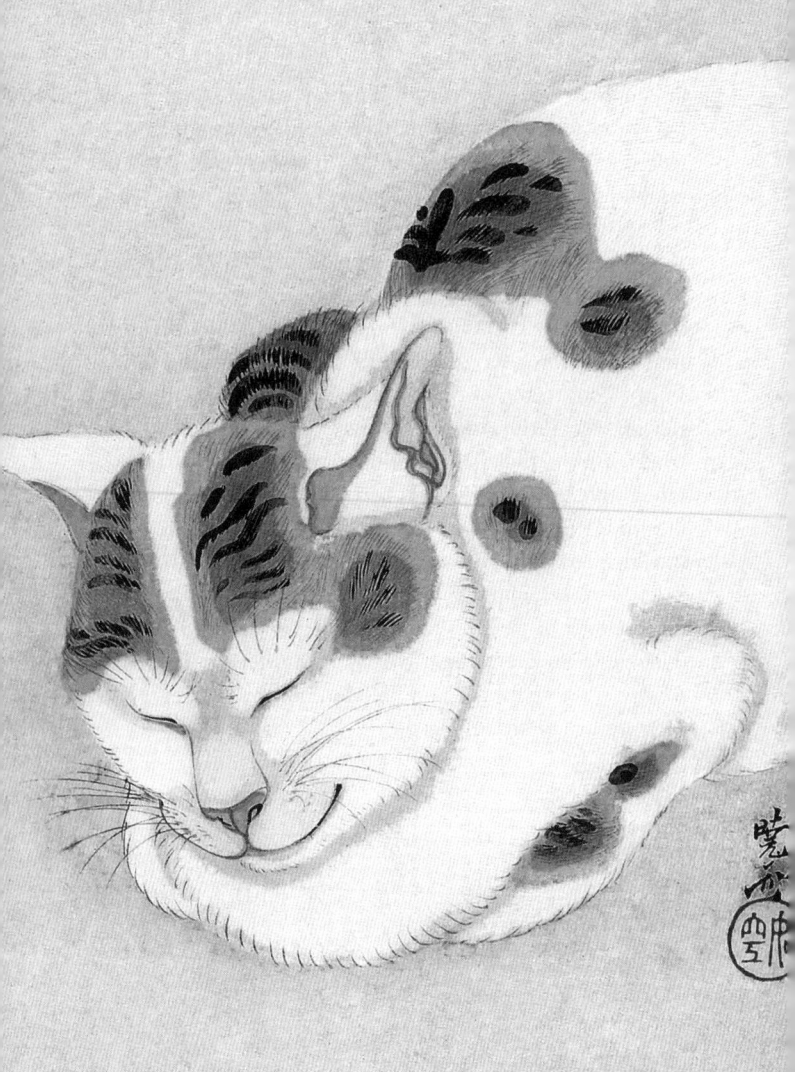

1| Katsushika Hokusai

Resting cats, around 1814–1819,
detail of a panel from the Manga
22.7 × 15.8 cm

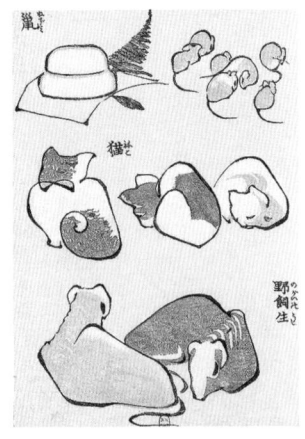

2| Takahashi Shotei

Tama, 1926
23.5 × 33.3 cm

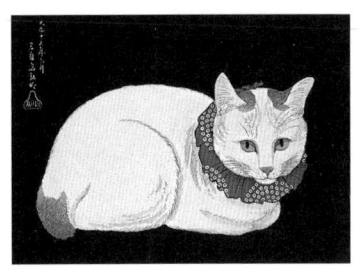

3| Takahashi Shotei

Playing Cats, around 1930

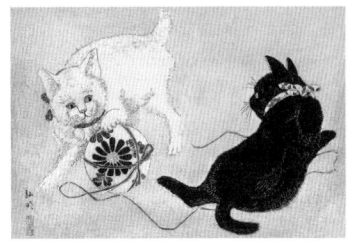

4| Tsukioka Yoshitoshi

*Young Woman from Kansei Period
Playing with Her Cat*, 1888
From the series: *Thirty-two Aspects of
Customs and Manners*
37 × 25,4 cm

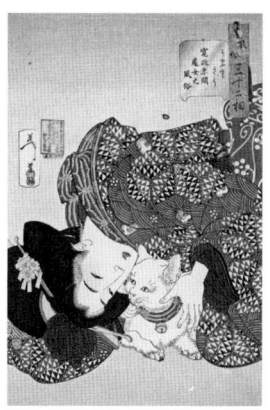

**5| Utagawa Hiroshige II,
aka Shigenobu**

A White Cat Playing with a String, 1863
21.3 × 26.7 cm

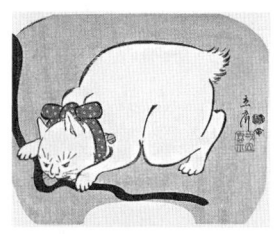

6| Utagawa Kuniyoshi

Woman Playing with Cat, Fishmonger and Dog,
ca. 1821–1823
From the series:
Sundial of Modern Tradesmen: Noon
39.5 × 26.7 cm

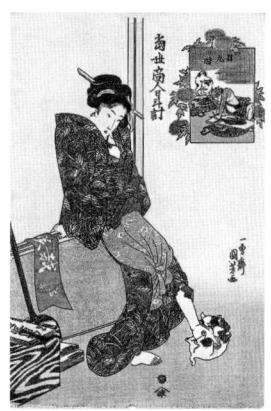

7| Utagawa Kunisada

Cat and Beauty, between 1818 and 1830
From a series of three triptychs:
Beauties in New Styles Dyed to Order

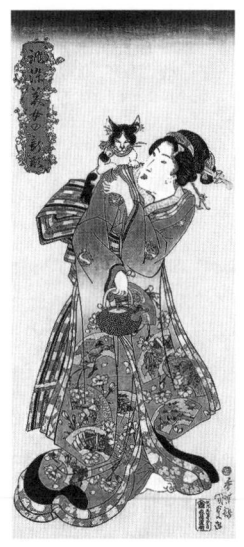

8| Utagawa Sadakage I

The Pride of Edo: an Assortment of Beauties,
around 1830
37 × 78 cm (triptych)

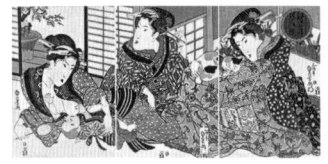

9| Takahashi Shotei

Cat with Bell, around 1935
26.99 × 39.37 cm

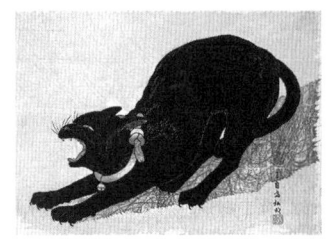

10| Utagawa Yoshifuji

The Head of the Cat-witch of Okabe,
around 1847–1848
From the series: *Cats Suggested as the*
Fifty-three Stations of the Tōkaidō Road
36.7 × 25.5 cm

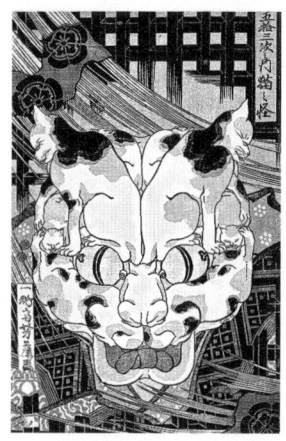

11| Utagawa Yoshifuji

Assemblage of Kittens Form a Mother Cat,
around *1847–1852*

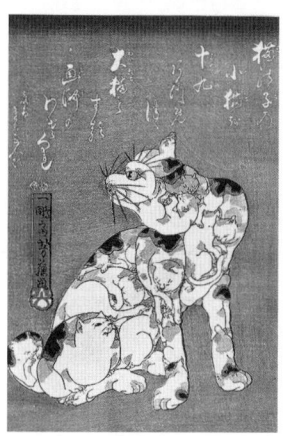

12| Utagawa Kunisada

The Head of the Cat-Witch of Okabe,
detail of a triptych: *The Village of Yatsuhashi*
at Okasaki, 1835
From the series: *Cats Suggested as*
the Fifty-three Stations of the Tōkaidō Road
(triptych)

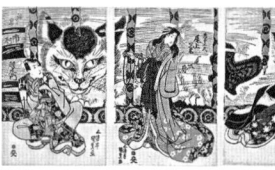

13| Utagawa Kuniyoshi

The Cat-Witch of Okabe, 1847
From the series: *Cats Suggested as the
Fifty-three Stations of the Tōkaidō Road*
36.6 × 73.8 cm (triptych)

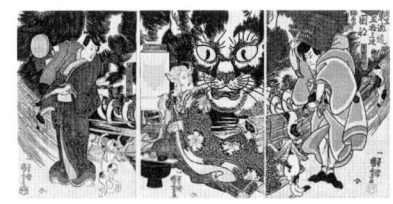

14| Utagawa Kuniyoshi

*Cats Suggested as the Fifty-three Stations
of the Tōkaidō Road*, circa 1847–1850
35.4 × 23.9 cm
(each plate, triptych)

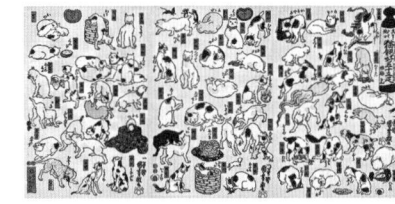

15| Utagawa Kuniyoshi

Proverbs Illustrated by Cats,
around 1852
35.2 × 24.4 cm
(each plate, triptych)

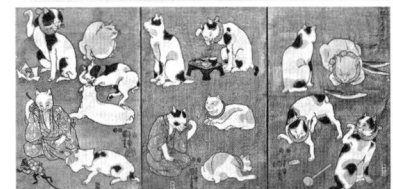

16| Utagawa Kuniyoshi

*Cats Forming the Hiragana Characters
for Bonito*, circa 1842
From the series: *Cats Forming Characters*
36.2 × 25.3 cm

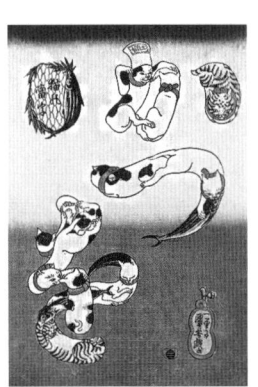

17| Utagawa Kuniyoshi

Pale Moon, Cats in Season, 1846
(*uchiwa* fan)
22.4 × 28.8 cm

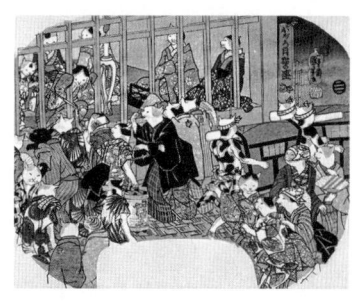

18| Utagawa Kuniyoshi

*Anthropomorphic Cats Relaxing
in Summer,* around 1842 (*uchiwa* fan)
22.4 × 28.7 cm

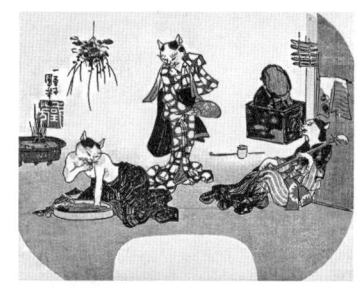

19| Toyohara Chikanobu

Cats on a Roof, around 1900
32 × 21.6 cm

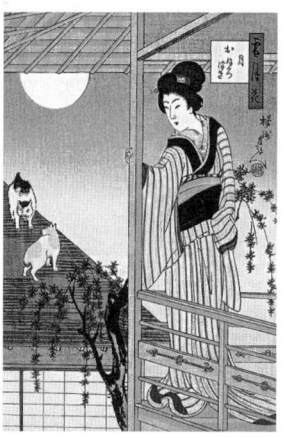

20| Utagawa Hiroshige

Asakusa Ricefields and Torinomachi Festival,
around 1857
From the series:
One Hundred Famous Views of Edo, no. 101
33.7 × 22.7 cm

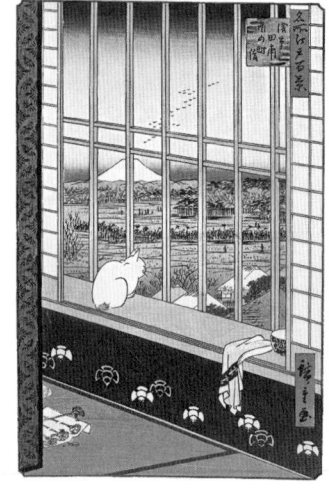

21| Suzuki Harunobu

Two Lovers with Cat by a Bonsai and Plum,
18th century

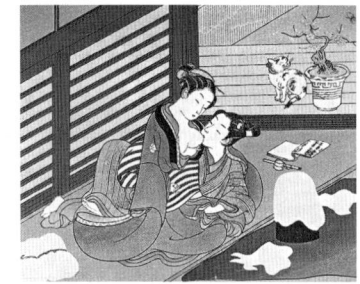

22| Katsukawa Shunshō

Lovers with a Cat, 1788 Ninth print in a series
of twelve prints titled
The Haikai Book of the Cuckoo or
Worshipping a Woman's Pussy at Night

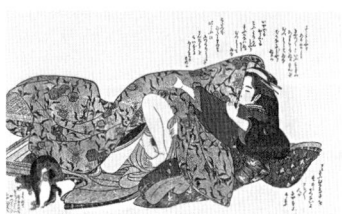

23| Suzuki Harunobu

Calligraphy Teacher and Pupil
with Mating Cats, 1770
From the series:
The Amorous Adventures of Mane'emon
20.6 × 28.5 cm

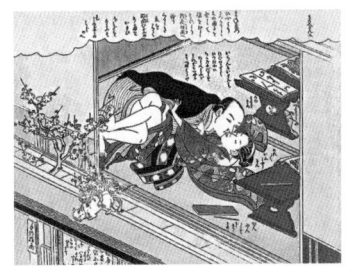

24| Kitagawa Utamaro

A Woman and a Cat (parody of the third
princess Onna San No Miya),
1793–1794
38.4 × 25.9 cm

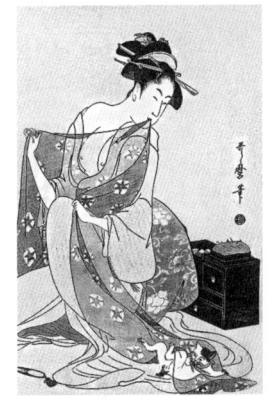

25| Suzuki Harunobu

Onna San no Miya (the Third Princess),
around 1768–1770
(illustration from The Tale of Genji)
26.2 × 19.2 cm

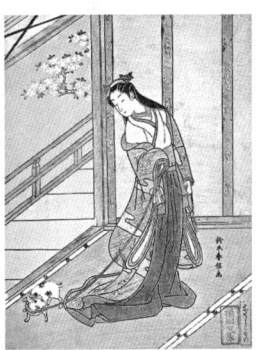

26 | Yanagawa Shigenobu II

Geisha Tuning her Shamisen
21.4 × 19.1 cm

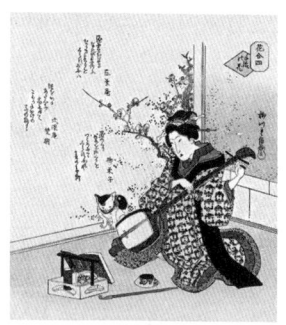

27 | Kitagawa Utamaro

The Courtesan Hanaōgi of Ōgiya,
around 1801
From the series:
Six Flowers of the Yoshiwara
37.2 × 25.2 cm

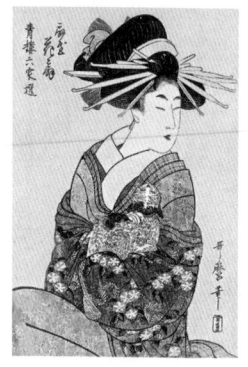

28 | Chōkōsai Eishō

Motozue of the Daimonjiya,
around 1795–1797
From the series: *Contest of
Beauties of the Pleasure Quarters*
38.5 × 25.7 cm

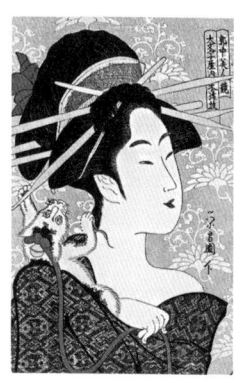

29| Toyohara Kunichika

Geisha of Yanagibashi,
1870 From the series:
Thirty-six Restaurants of Tokyo

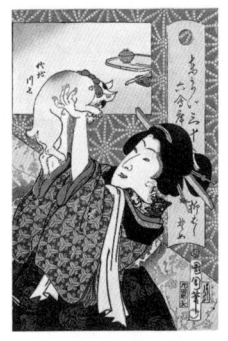

30| Utagawa Kunisada

Beauty and Cat,
between 1843 and 1847 *(kakemono)*
From the series: *Fabrics Woven
to Order for Modern Taste*
65.3 × 22 cm
(diptych, right-hand print)

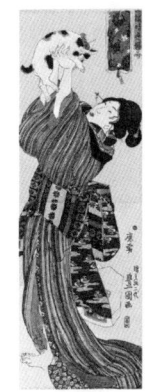

31| Takahashi Shotei

Black Cat and Tomato Plant, 1931
53 × 37.6 cm

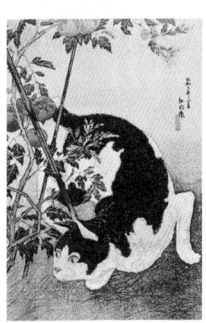

32| Utagawa Kunisada

Woman Dressing her Daughter's Hair,
around 1830
From the series: *Fashionable Twelve
Months, tenth month*
36.6 × 25.4 cm

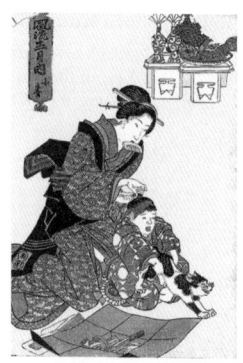

33| Ohara Koson

Cat and Bowl of Goldfish,
1931

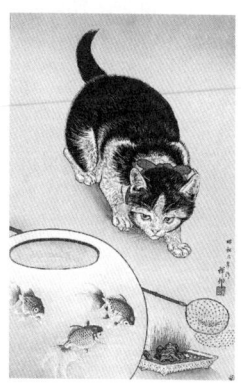

34| Ohara Koson

Cat Catching a Mouse,
around 1930
33.3 × 24 cm

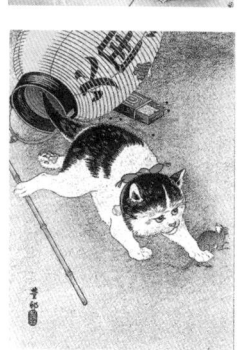

35| Ohara Koson

Cat and Goldfish,
around 1928–1930
27 × 40.8 cm

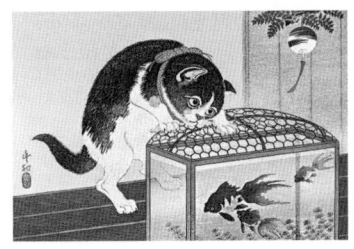

36| Kobayashi Kiyochika

Cat and Lantern, 1877
30.7 × 43.5 cm

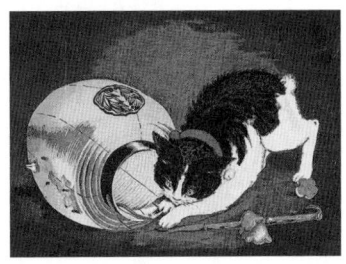

37| Utagawa Kuniyoshi

Amusements of the First Snowfall,
1847–1852
36.5 × 73 cm (triptych)

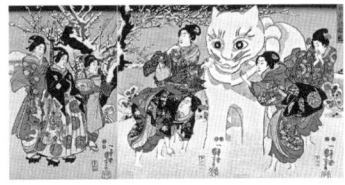

38| Suzuki Harunobu

Tickling Her Foot,
around 1765–1770
25.7 × 20.8 cm

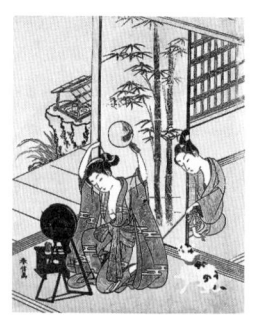

39| Utagawa Kunisada

Woman Playing with Cat, around 1820
From the series:
Spring Dawn: A Contest of Beauties
36.3 × 26 cm

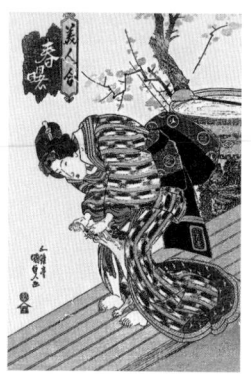

40| Kitagawa Utamaro

Wild Chrysanthemum: Women and Cat,
around 1795 From the series: *Renowned
beauties likened to the Six Immortal Poets*
24.5 × 18 cm

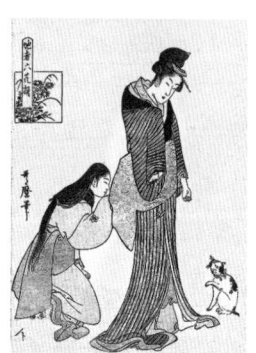

41| Miyagawa Issho

Courtesan Playing with a Cat
From the series: *Thirty-two Aspects of Customs and Manners*
8.8 × 13.8 cm

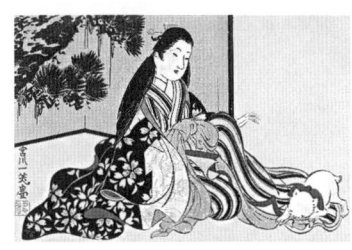

42| Utagawa Kuniyoshi

Kneeling Woman Spinning in Front of a Screen with a Cat Sleeping Behind Her, around 1843
Instructive Index of All Sorts of Proverbs
36.4 × 25.3 cm

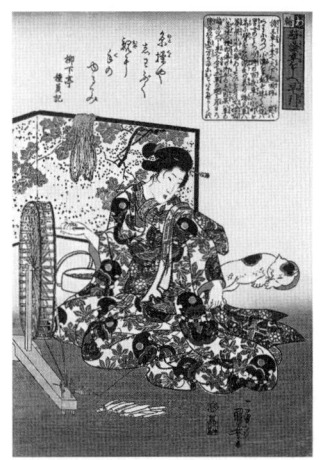

43| Utagawa Kuniyoshi

Chrysanthemums, 1844–1848
(*uchiwa* fan)
From the series: *Eight Selected Flowers from the Garden*

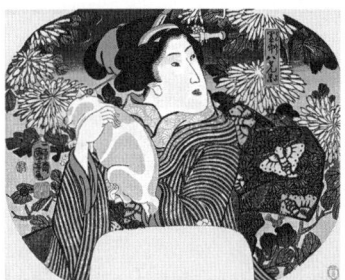

44| Utagawa Kuniyoshi

Woman Playing with Cat, around 1845
22.8 × 28.8 cm (fan)

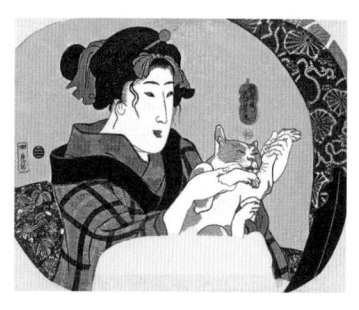

45| Isoda Koryusai

Cat Pawing at Goldfish,
around 1770–1780
24.5 × 19.2 cm

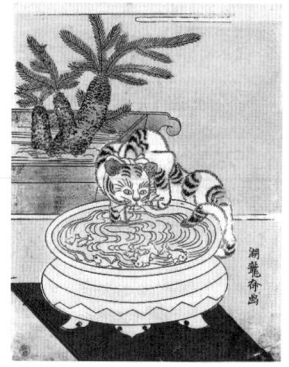

46| Isoda Koryusai

Puppies and Narcissus in the Snow,
circa 1773
26.3 × 19.6 cm

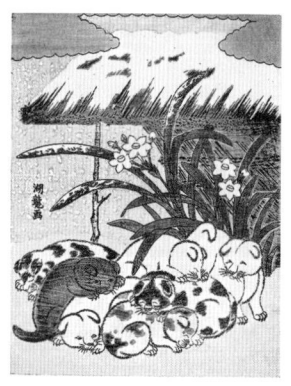

47| Utagawa Kunimasa

Woman, Cat and Kotatsu, 1796
36.5 × 24.5 cm

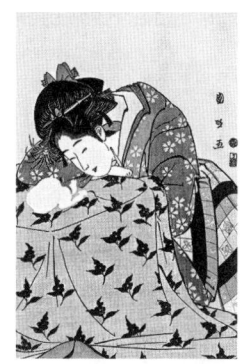

48| Toyohara Chikanobu

*Two Geishas Relaxing After Having
Entertained a Client,* 1888

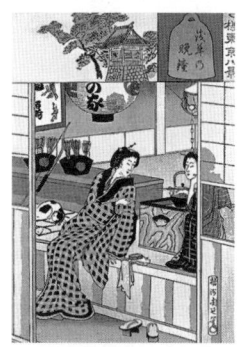

49| Toyohara Chikanobu

Women Raising Silkworms,
around 1880

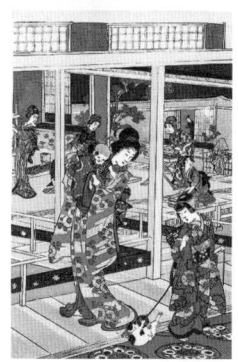

50| Teisai Sencho

Emon of the Maru-Ebiya
From the series: *Comparisons of
Courtesans and Flowers*
35.8 × 24.5 cm

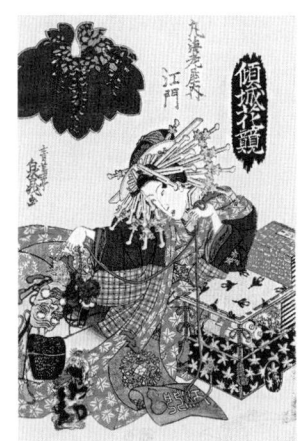

51| Utagawa Kunisada

*Parody of the Third Princess Onna San
No Miya and Kashiwagi,* 1858
Illustration of The Tale of Genji
36.2 × 24.8 cm
(each plate of the diptych)

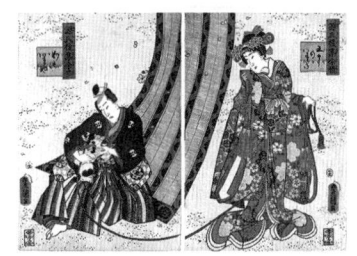

52| Kitagawa Utamaro

Courtesan with Cat, around 1790
25.8 × 37 cm

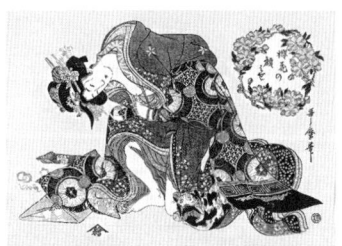

53| Utagawa Kuniyoshi

Brazier (Kotatsu), around 1827–1830
From the series: *Fashionable Women as
the One Hundred and Eight Heroes
of the Suikoden*
20.9 × 18.3 cm

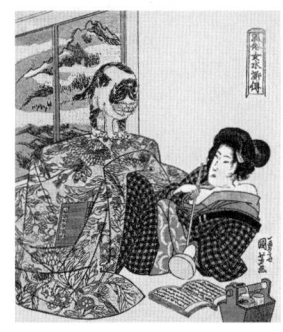

54| Utagawa Kunisada

Shaving the Nape of the Neck,
around 1819–1820
From the series: *Modern Eastern
Brocade Prints*
36.8 × 26 cm

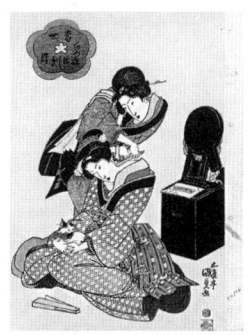

55| Utagawa Kuniyoshi

*"Oh, it hurts!" and Giant Octopus from
the Nameri River in Etchu,*
around 1852
From the series: *The Celebrated
Treasures of Mountains and Seas*
37.8 × 25.6 cm

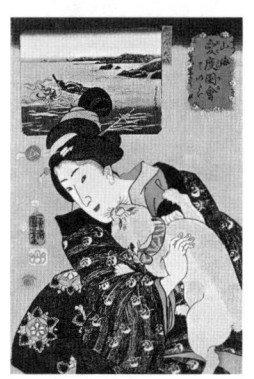

56| Utagawa Kuniyoshi

Woman Reading, 1852
From the series: *The Celebrated
Treasures of Mountains and Seas*
35.5 × 24.8 cm

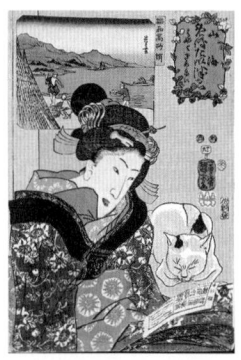

57| Tsukioka Yoshitoshi

Lady Tenshōin, 1886
Personalities of Recent Times,
supplement (furoku)
to the *Yamato Shimbun* newspaper
39.4 × 26.7 cm

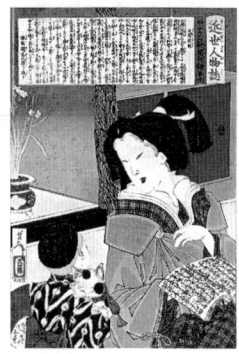

58| Utagawa Kuniyoshi

Komachi Prays for Rain, 1854
37.7 × 25.5 cm

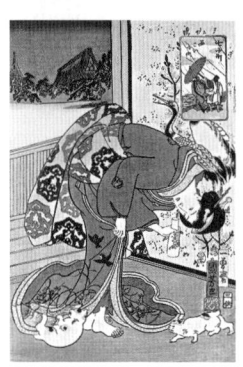

59| Tsukioka Yoshitoshi

The Courtesan Usugumo Holding a Cat,
around 1876
From the series:
*A Mirror of Beauties of
the Past and Present*
39.4 × 26.7 cm

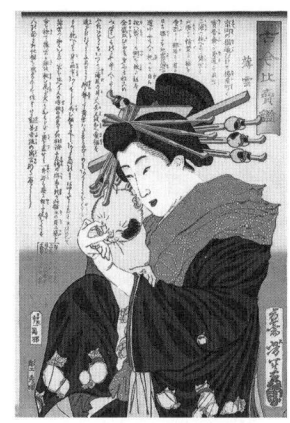

60| Tsukioka Yoshitoshi

*Fukusuke of Shimbashi with Morning
Glories at Iriya,* 1880
From the series: *Pride of Tokyo's
Twelve Months; June*

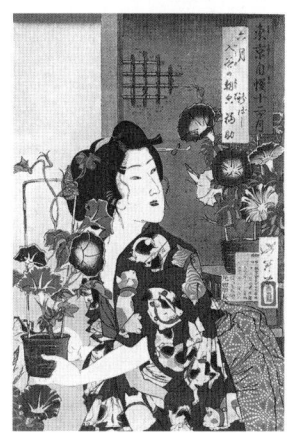

61| Katsushika Hokusai

Cat and Butterfly, 1839 Detail
of a manuscript scroll decorated
with various drawings
37.2 × 1,434 cm (whole roll)

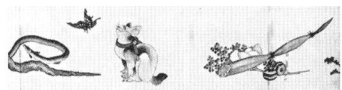

62| Toyohara Kunichika

Woman Playing with Cat, 1865
From the series: *Thirty-six Elegant
Selections of Charming Figures*
37 × 25 cm

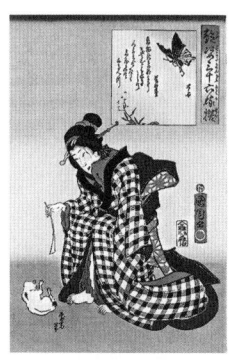

63| Keisai Eisen

*Pine Tree of the Myôken Hall in
Yanagishima: Woman Playing with Cat*
38 × 25.5 cm

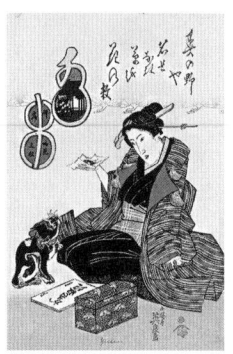

64| Tsukioka Yoshitoshi

*I Want to Cancel My Subscription
(Woman Reading a Newspaper)*, 1878
From the series: *Collection of Desires*
39.4 × 26.7 cm

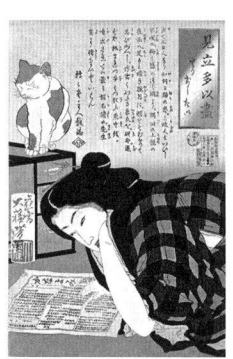

65| Keisai Eisen

Clearing Weather at Nakamichi, late 1820s
From the series:
Eight Dates with Geisha – Eight Views on Fans
37 × 24.8 cm

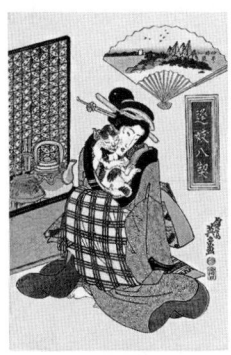

66| Utagawa Kuniyoshi

Cat to Keep Mice Away,
around 1842

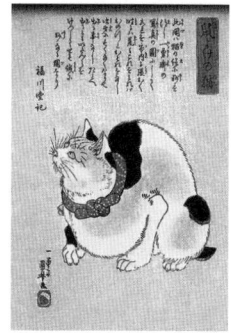

67| Toshikata Mizuno

Merchant's Daughter, 1900
13.8 × 8.8 cm

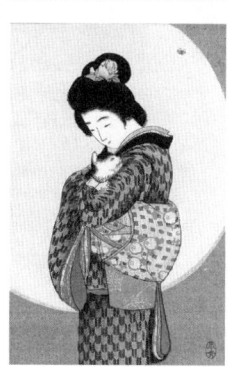

68| Ikeda Shoen

Young Woman with Cat, 1907 Published
in *Jogaku Sekai*, a women's magazine
published by Hakubunkan in Tokyo,
from 1901 to 1925
13.8 × 8.8 cm

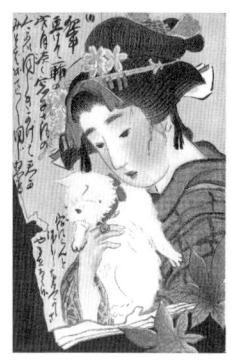

69| Utagawa Kuniyoshi

Whetstone, 1843–1847
From the series:
Index of Representative Proverbs
37.3 × 25.7 cm

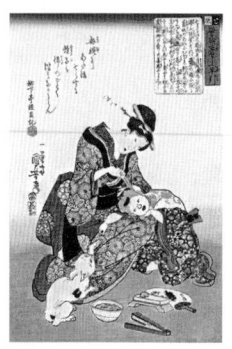

70| Toshikata Mizuno

*After the Bath: Woman of
the Kansei Era*, 1894
From the series: *Thirty-six Elegant
Selections of Charming Figures*
35.2 × 24 cm

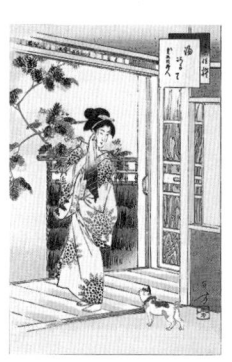

71| Toyohara Chikanobu

Playing with Cat, 1897
From the series:
True Beauties, based on a series by Utamaro
35 × 25 cm

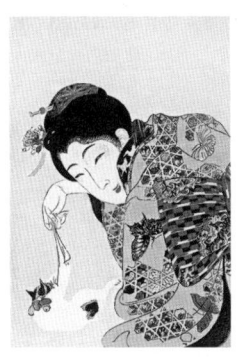

72| Toyohara Chikanobu

Azuma – Playing with Kitten, 1896
35.5 × 24.4 cm

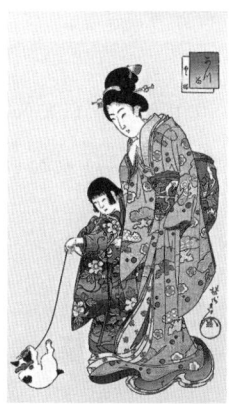

73| Totoya Hokkei

Cat Playing with a Toy Butterfly, surimono,
around 1825
From the series: *A Collection of
Thirty-Six Birds and Animals*
21.2 × 17.7 cm

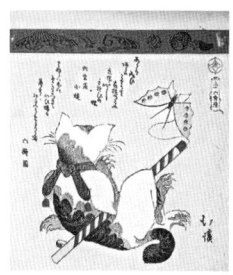

74| Kawanabe Kyōsai

Cat and Mouse, around 1870
37.5 × 25.1 cm

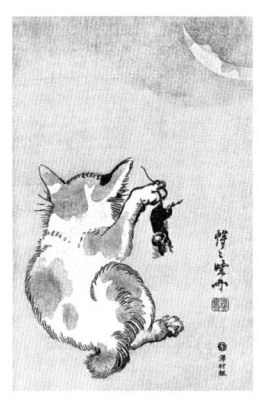

75| Kobayashi Kiyochika

Backgammon and Musashi, 1894
From the series: *Children's games*

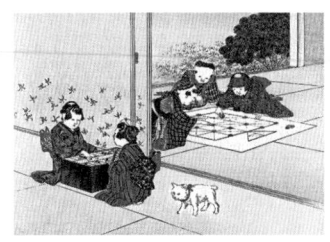

76| Kawanabe Kyosai

Sleeping Cat, around 1885–1889
23.8 × 24.1 cm

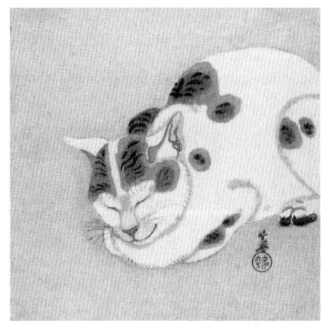

The great masters of printmaking
presented in this book

Miyagawa Issho (1689–1779)
Suzuki Harunobu (1725 ? –1770)
Katsukawa Shunshō (1726–1792)
Isoda Koryusai (1735–1790)
Kitagawa Utamaro (1753–1806)
Katsushika Hokusai (1760–1849)
Utagawa Toyokuni (1769–1825)
Utagawa Kunimasa (1773–1810)
Totoya Hokkei (1780–1850)
Utagawa Kunisada (Toyokuni III, 1786–1865)
Yanagawa Shigenobu (1787–1832/1833)
Keisai Eisen (1790–1848)
Utagawa Hiroshige (1797–1858)
Utagawa Kuniyoshi (1798–1861)
Teisai Sencho (active from 1830 to 1850)
Utagawa Sadakage I (active from 1818 to 1844)
Hiroshige II (1826–1869)
Utagawa Yoshifuji (1828–1887)
Kawanabe Kyōsai (1831–1889)
Toyohara Kunichika (1835–1900)
Toyohara Chikanobu (1838–1912)
Tsukioka Yoshitoshi (1839–1892)
Utagawa Yoshitaki (1841–1899)
Kobayashi Kiyochika (1843–1915)
Toshikata Mizuno (1866–1908)
Takahashi Hiroaki aka Shotei (1871–1945)
Ohara Koson (1877–1945)
Ikeda Shoen (1886–1917)

Photographic credits (The numbers refer to those of the images.)

Alamy Bilddatenbank / Universal Images Group North America LLC: 44

Art Institute of Chicago / Clarence Buckingham Collection: 46; / Gift of Helen C. Gunsaulus: 73 | **Bridgeman Images:** 12; / Pictures from History: 1, 21, 28, 48, 66; / © Oriental Museum, Durham University: 71; Photo © Christie's Images: 26 / © Mead Art Museum / Gift of William Green: 10; / Stefano Bianchetti: 11; / Molteni & Motta/UIG: 15, 17, 18, 55; / © Fitzwilliam Museum: 53; / © Edinburgh University Library / With kind permission of the University of Edinburgh: 75 | **Bridgeman Images / Photograph © 2021 Museum of Fine Arts, Boston**. All rights reserved / William Sturgis Bigelow Collection: 6, 13, 28, 37, 40, 50, 69; / Nellie Parney Carter Collection – Bequest of Nellie Parney Carter: 8; / William S. and John T. Spaulding Collection: 27, 47; / Leonard A. Lauder Collection of Japanese Postcards: 41; / Nellie Parney Carter Collection – Bequest of Nellie Parney Carter: 54 | **Edo-Tokyo-Museum:** 72 | **Harvard Art Museums** / Arthur M. Sacxkler Museum, Gift of Dr. Denman W. Ross: 30; / Gift of the Friends of Arthur B. Duel: 45 | **Lacma, Los Angeles** / Gift of Mr. and Mrs. Felix Juda: 9, 31 | **MAK – Museum für angewandte Kunst, Wien:** 39 | **Minneapolis Institute of Arts** / Bequest of Richard P. Gale: 5; / Gift of Paul Schweitzer: 35; / Gift of Louis W. Hill, Jr.: 23, 25, 29, 76 | **Philadelphia Museum of Art** / Purchased with funds contributed by the E. Rhodes and Leona B. Carpenter Foundation, 1989: 57, 59, 64 | **Photo © RMN-Grand Palais (MNAAG, Paris)** / Thierry Ollivier (Paris, Musée Guimet – Nationales Museum der asiatischen Künste): 52 | **Rijksmuseum, Amsterdam:** 14 | **Smithsonian Institution, Washington** / Robert O. Muller Collection: 2, 19, 34, 36, 74; / Gift of Alan, Donald, and David Winslow from the estate of William R. Castle: 20 | **The British Museum, London:** © The Trustees of the British Museum: 23, 38, 42, 56, 58 | **The Metropolitan Museum of Art, New York** / Gift of Lincoln Kirstein, 1985: 4; / H. O. Havemeyer Collection, Bequest of Mrs. H. O. Havemeyer, 1929: 24, 25; / Gift of Lincoln Kirstein, 1985: 51 | **Tokyo Metro Library:** 70

© Prestel Verlag,
Munich · London · New York, 2024
Third edition 2025

produktsicherheit@penguinrandomhouse.de
(The above information is mandatory information according to GPSR and should be
used for all queries relating to the safety of
our books)

Prestel Verlag
A member of Penguin Random House
Verlagsgruppe GmbH
Neumarkter Strasse 28 · 81673 Munich

The publisher expressly reserves the right to
exploit the copyrighted content of this work
for the purposes of text and data mining in
accordance with Section 44b of the German
Copyright Act (UrhG), based on the
European Digital Single Market Directive.
Any unauthorized use is an infringement of
copyright and is hereby prohibited.

A CIP catalogue record for this book is
available from the British Library.

The French original edition was published by
Édition Hazan as Les Chats
© Éditions Hazan, 2022

Translation
David Rocher

Proofreading
John Stilwell

Production
Martina Effaga

Typesetting
Weiß-Freiburg GmbH,
Grafik und Buchgestaltung

Lithographie
Litho Art New, Turin, Italy

Printing and binding
Toppan Leefung Printing

Printed in China

ISBN 978-3-7913-7720-9

www.prestel.com